OVER LAND

Inventions are designed to make our lives easier and sometimes more enjoyable, whether it's moving around, entertaining ourselves or even saving lives. People have come up with many ingenious ways to travel over land safely, easily and quickly from place to place, and maybe even have some fun on the way!

People power!

During the first half of the 19th century, two-wheeled human-powered vehicles became popular. They were produced in many designs, including penny-farthings, which have a huge front wheel attached directly to the pedals. The first modern bicycle designs appeared towards the end of the 1800s.

In 1876, German inventor Nikolaus Otto developed the four-stroke internal combustion engine. This power source has been used to drive cars and other motor vehicles for more than 100 years.

KARL BENZ

In 1885, Karl Benz (1844–1929) fitted a motor engine to a three-wheeled carriage, inventing the car in the process.

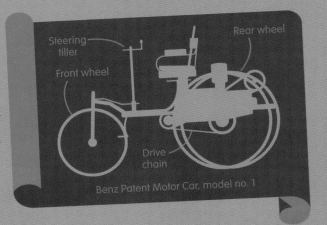

Steering tiller

Rear wheel

Front wheel

Drive chain

Benz Patent Motor Car, model no. 1

Any colour, as long as it's black

I'm Henry Ford (1863–1947). I'm an industrialist from the USA, and in 1913 I introduced a moving conveyor belt to my car factory to speed up manufacture. At its peak, my factory was producing a Ford Model T car every 10 seconds.

HENRY FORD

Road safety

These features and inventions have helped to make driving far safer today than it has ever been:

1800s – seat belts are invented, but they are not introduced until the late 1940s.

1903 – Mary Anderson invents the first windscreen wipers.

1934 – English inventor, Percy Shaw, patents cat's eyes – special reflective devices used to mark out roads.

1949 – The first crash test dummies are used.

1953 – John W Hetrick from the USA invents the airbag.

1960s – Anti-lock brake systems are introduced to road vehicles.

Q: What's the fastest production car in the world?

A: The Bugatti Chiron has a top speed of 420 kph, but that's limited because the manufacturer believes that tyres can't cope with faster speeds. In theory, it could reach 463 kph!

In the late 1940s, surfers in California, USA, wanted a way of keeping busy when the waves were flat. They fixed wheels to short boards and started 'sidewalk surfing' – and skateboarding was born.

In September 2017, Peter Connolly of the UK set a speed record on a skateboard in a standing position – he zoomed to 146.73 kph!

INTO THE AIR AND BEYOND

People have been dreaming of flying for thousands of years. However, getting off the ground takes a little more effort and invention than just flapping your arms, as these intrepid inventors discovered.

Gliding through the air

During the 1800s, English inventor George Cayley wrote about and built the first working gliders. But he wasn't brave enough to test them himself and chose a small local boy and even his own butler, John Appleby, to try out his flying machines.

Cayley's glider

Towards the end of the 1800s, some inventors, such as Félix du Temple from France, tried to fly steam-powered aircraft.

In 1903, Orville Wright (1871–1948) and Wilbur Wright (1867–1912) from the USA became the first people to build and fly a powered, controlled aircraft. Their first flight lasted a whole 12 seconds and covered just 37 m.

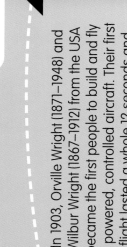

1969 – Neil Armstrong (1930–2012) becomes the first person to step on the Moon, having been blasted there in a Saturn V rocket designed by von Braun.

1961 – Yuri Gagarin (1934–1968) becomes the first person in space.

Steps into space

1957 – Sputnik becomes the first human-made object to orbit Earth.

1944 – V2 rockets, designed by German engineer Wernher von Braun, are used in warfare for the first time.

1926 – American inventor Robert Goddard builds the first liquid-fuelled rocket, which flies for just 2.5 seconds.

In comparison, the longest commercial airline flight is between Singapore in Southeast Asia and Newark, New Jersey, USA. It covers more than 15,300 km and can take nearly 19 hours.

Heinkel He178

In the 1920s and 1930s, two inventors separately developed the first jet engines. Frank Whittle from England was the first to patent his in 1930 and test one in 1937, but German Hans von Ohain was the first to see his engine fly when the jet-powered Heinkel He178 took to the skies in August 1939.

Breakthroughs in flight

• Want to know how high you are? Then you've got to thank German inventor Paul Kollsman. In 1928, he developed the first barometric altimeter.

• If you really want to get above it all, then you need a pressurised cabin, otherwise a lot more than your ears would go pop! In 1938, the first airliner Boeing 307, the first airliner with a pressurised cabin, entered service.

• In 1952, the first commercial jetliner, the de Havilland Comet, entered service.

• The Antonov AN-225 – the heaviest plane ever – makes its first flight in 1988.

FRANK WHITTLE

HANS VON OHAIN

OVER AND UNDER WATER

Whether it's cruising over the water's surface or exploring underwater, these inventions were created to make moving through the water quick and easy.

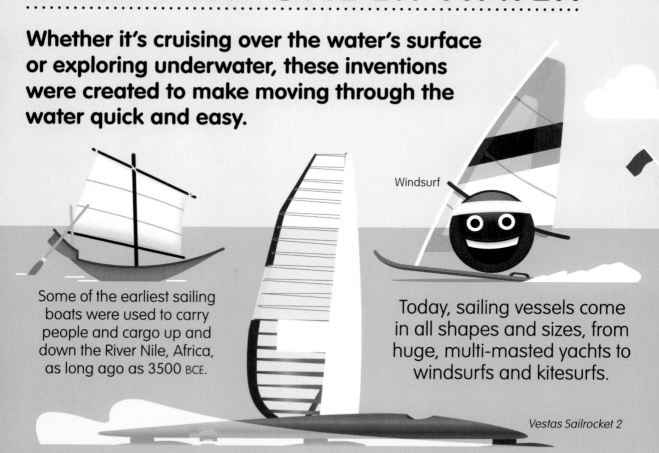

Windsurf

Some of the earliest sailing boats were used to carry people and cargo up and down the River Nile, Africa, as long ago as 3500 BCE.

Today, sailing vessels come in all shapes and sizes, from huge, multi-masted yachts to windsurfs and kitesurfs.

Vestas Sailrocket 2

The sailing speed record was set in 2012 by Australian Paul Larsen in his yacht *Vestas Sailrocket 2*. He reached a speed of 65.45 knots.

In 1624, Dutch inventor Cornelis Drebbel launched an oar-powered submarine that sailed on and under the River Thames, in London, UK.

SS *Great Britain*

English engineer Isambard Kingdom Brunel (1806–1859) was responsible for many transport inventions and developments, including groundbreaking designs of dockyards and railways. In 1843, he oversaw the building of the SS *Great Britain*, the world's first ocean-going, propeller-driven, iron ship (and also the largest ship ever built to that point).

ISAMBARD KINGDOM BRUNEL

Great boating inventions

Magnetic compass – invented in China around 200 BCE.

Screw propeller – developed by British inventor Francis Pettit Smith in 1836.

Radar – first developed in 1934 by the US Naval Research Laboratory.

In 1775, David Bushnell (1740–1824) of America built the first submarine to be used in war. The next year, *The Turtle* was used against British ships during the American War of Independence (1775–1783).

Take a deep breath

In 1943, French scientists Jacques Cousteau (1910–1997) and Émile Gagnan (1900–1979) developed an underwater breathing system. This breathing apparatus, or Aqua-Lung, had a tank of compressed air that was fed to the diver through a special valve, allowing a person to explore the underwater world outside a submarine or submersible.

SAVING LIVES

The inventions on these pages have helped doctors and medics diagnose and treat harmful conditions and diseases. As a result, they have saved millions of lives of people all around the world.

Q: How can we see inside a body?

A: X-rays are one way. They can create a picture of the hard parts of the body, such as bones, or parts that have been dyed using special chemicals.

In 1895, German scientist, I, Wilhelm Röntgen (1845–1923), found that some waves of energy passed through soft body parts, but were stopped by hard body parts. I used a photographic plate and made the first X-ray image – a picture of the bones in my wife's hand.

WILHELM RÖNTGEN

Other scanning steps

1957 – Researchers at the University of Alabama, USA, develop the optic endoscope. It uses thin tubes with glass fibres, which can carry video signals through a small opening in the body.

1971 – British engineer Godfrey Hounsfield invented CT (computerised tomography) scanners, which use lots of different X-rays to build up a 3D picture.

1977 – Raymond Damadian invents the MRI (magnetic resonance imaging) machine, which uses radio waves to build up a picture of the inside of the body.

Keep it clean
In 1865, I, Joseph Lister (1827–1912), discovered that cleaning wounds would kill bacteria and help to prevent infections. I used a chemical called phenol, or carbolic acid, which became the first antiseptic.

JOSEPH LISTER

Sticking plasters were invented in 1920 by Earle Dickson. He cut up small pieces of bandage and added sticking tape to make them easy to fix and hold in place.

In 1928, Alexander Fleming (1881–1955) noticed that spores of a mold, called penicillin, killed off or stopped the growth of disease-causing bacteria. He had discovered the first antibiotics that are now used to treat and stop the spread of infections.

A vaccination is a type of medicine that contains a harmless form of a disease. It helps the body acquire an immunity against that disease. In 1796, English doctor Edward Jenner (1749–1823) tested the first vaccination by giving a boy called James Phipps cowpox, which is a harmless form of smallpox. The smallpox virus was responsible for killing as much as 20 per cent of all people living in towns at the time.

Caring for the sick
Florence Nightingale (1820–1910) is considered the inventor of modern nursing. During the Crimean War (1853–1856), she organised care for the wounded and after the war she established one of the first nursing schools in the world at St Thomas' hospital in London.

FLORENCE NIGHTINGALE

BUILDING A BETTER WORLD

Whether you want a large monument that will last for thousands of years, a super-tall building that will stretch into the sky or the latest technology to harness renewable energy, then these are the inventions for you!

More than 2,000 years ago, the Romans started to use concrete to construct large buildings. What made their concrete mix special was the use of a type of volcanic ash that made the concrete hard-wearing and able to set quickly, even when submerged in water.

Colosseum

Pantheon

The Romans used concrete to build public baths, harbours, piers, and large buildings such as the Pantheon, the Forum and the Colosseum in Rome.

Other Roman building innovations included more than 80,000 km of arrow-straight roads and the use of arches in the building of monuments, bridges and buildings.

Completed in 1884, Chicago's 12-storey, 55-metre tall Home Insurance Building is considered the world's first skyscraper. In comparison, the tallest building in the world today, the Burj Khalifa in Dubai is 828 metres tall and has 163 floors above ground level.

Burj Khalifa

Reach for the sky

During the 19th century, a number of inventions and developments allowed architects to create buildings that stretched up to the sky.

Bessemer steel, rolled into I-shaped beams, allowed for stronger and taller frames than those using older cast iron.

Sprinkler systems meant that tall buildings, if fitted with them, no longer faced the threat of devastating fires.

In 1852, Elisha Otis invented the safety elevator, which stopped the elevator dropping if the cable broke.

I demonstrated my safety elevator by riding one high above a watching crowd, and then cutting the cable!

ELISHA OTIS

At the cutting edge

Some of the latest innovations in building technology look to harness new sources of energy. They include:

Photovoltaic glazing – special windows that include solar cells to produce electricity.

Kinetic pavements – special sections of pavement that generate electricity as people walk over them.

Self-healing concrete – a type of concrete that uses bacteria, inside tiny capsules, which produce limestone to close a crack when water enters it.

IN THE KITCHEN

Look around your kitchen and you'll see that it's packed with gadgets, gizmos and equipment to help you cook and prepare your food, making it tasty and safe to eat.

My name is Josephine Cochrane, and in 1887, I had become so tired of my crockery being chipped and broken by clumsy servants, that I invented a practical dishwashing machine. It used a wire frame to hold dishes and a copper boiler with a wooden wheel that was turned around to cover the dishes with hot, soapy water.

JOSEPHINE COCHRANE

Fancy a quick, tasty snack? – then you can thank US factory mechanic Charles Strite, who invented the pop-up toaster in 1919.

He used a timer that activated a set of springs to pop the toast out when it was done.

While working in Canada in 1912, Clarence Birdseye noticed how fish that had frozen quickly after it had been caught stayed fresh for a long time. In 1925, he invented a process that could freeze food quickly, bringing frozen food to billions of people.

Microwave cooking was discovered by accident! US engineer Percy Spencer was working on high-energy vacuum tubes called magnetrons in 1945, when he noticed that a chocolate bar in his pocket had melted.

Interested by this, he also tried an egg, which exploded! He realised that the microwaves given off by the magnetrons were cooking the food.

He patented the idea and built the first microwave oven the next year. But this huge device was nearly 1.8 metres tall, weighed 340 kg and cost nearly US$5,000 (that's about US$55,000 today!).

Keep it clean

In 1913, English metallurgist (metal specialist) Harry Brearley accidentally discovered that when he prepared metal alloys to study, he found a new type of chromium steel that was very resistant to staining and rust – stainless steel was born. Today, we use stainless steel for kitchen sinks and, of course, cutlery.

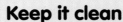

WARMTH AND LIGHT

For tens of thousands of years, flickering flames were the only way to warm and light the places we lived, worked and played in. Today, however, we have many different ways to bring light to the darkness and warmth to our homes.

Keeping warm

The Romans were clever people who built lots of things to make their lives easier and more comfortable. They developed one of the first forms of central heating. Called a hypocaust, it involved a large fire that heated air that would flow through a space under the floors, warming the rooms above.

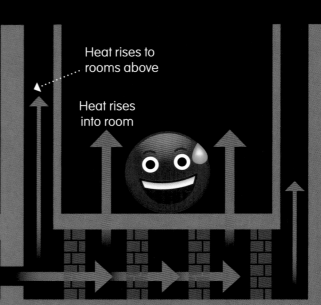

Heat rises to rooms above

Heat rises into room

Fire

Heat flowing under the floor

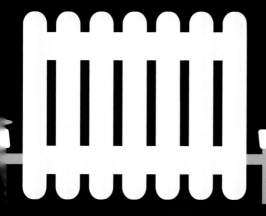

We had to wait for nearly 2,000 years for the development of modern central heating. In 1855, Russian inventor Franz San Galli developed the first radiators to warm buildings in the chilly city of St Petersburg, Russia.

Q: What did San Galli call his radiators?

A: He called them 'hot boxes' – not very imaginative!

Let there be light?

Q: Who invented the electric light bulb?

Filament

A: I did that! My name's Thomas Edison (1847–1931) and in 1879 I showed off the first electric light bulbs to the public and created a special filament that glowed for 1,200 hours.

THOMAS EDISON

Actually, nearly 20 years before Edison showed his light bulbs off, English scientist Joseph Swan (1828–1914) developed the first incandescent light bulb by putting a glowing filament in a vacuum. By 1881, his bulbs were used to light the Savoy Theatre in London, the first public building lit by electric lights.

In 1910, French engineer Georges Claude ran an electric current through neon gas, causing it to glow inside a glass tube, creating the first neon lights.

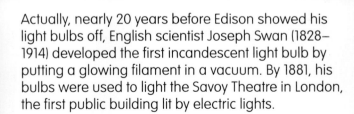

LEDs (light emitting diodes) are low-energy lights that are used in many modern homes and cars. But they were first described as long ago as the start of the 1900s and the first working LED was made by Russian inventor Oleg Losev in 1927.

KEEPING CLEAN

Getting rid of waste and keeping a place clean not only play key roles in making a home a nice place to live, they can also help to reduce the spread of diseases – and stop any nasty pongs!

When you've gotta go ...
Simple toilets have been used for more than 4,000 years. The ancient Minoans who lived on the island of Crete, Greece, had indoor toilets that were cleaned by hand using jugs of water or by small streams.

Round the bend
1596 – John Harington invented the first mechanical flushing toilet for his godmother, Queen Elizabeth I (1533–1603).

1775 – Alexander Cummings invented the S-bend, a curved pipe that stops smells coming out from the pipes.

Flushing toilets took a while to catch on, and for centuries people used a chamber pot kept under the bed. This was emptied every morning – usually out into the street – look out below!

Toilets in Japan take going to the loo to a whole different level. They can feature: washing facilities, air fresheners, heated seats, a noisemaker to drown out any embarrassing sounds, a self-washing bowl and even a remote control.

Spring clean!

Before the 1900s, cleaning the house involved a lot of hard work. Carpets and rugs had to be carried outside and hit with large beaters to knock out the dirt and dust.

In 1901, English inventor, Hubert Cecil Booth developed the first vacuum cleaner. It used an electric motor to suck air in and any dust with it. However, these early devices were huge and had to be parked outside a house with the tubes fed in through doors and windows.

American janitor, James Spangler, made the vacuum cleaner truly portable in 1907 when he combined a tin box with a brush, an electric fan and a pillow case to collect any dust. The next year, he sold the idea of his 'suction sweeper' to William Hoover.

The Electrolux Trilobite was the world's first robot vacuum cleaner. It was invented in 1997.

COMMUNICATION

The methods people use to pass information on to each other have changed dramatically over the years, from intricate glyphs and pictures that were carved onto stone to the modern alphabet and the latest electronic methods that can send messages at the speed of light.

Words and pictures
The oldest example of writing dates from about 3200 BCE. This early form of writing was called cuneiform and it used a series of wedge-shaped markings made into wet clay that was then baked hard. It was used throughout the Middle East.

Hieroglyphs are a system of pictures that were carved or painted onto walls or onto sheets of papyrus. The ancient Egyptians used them from about 3000 BCE onwards.

On the other side of the Atlantic in Central America, the Maya used a system of glyphs from about 300 BCE.

Around CE 105, Ts'ai Lun – an official at the Chinese Imperial Court – invented a form of paper using cloth and plant fibres that had been soaked, pressed and then dried to create a thin flat sheet that could be written on.

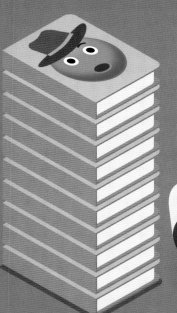

In 1450, German inventor Johannes Gutenberg (1394–1468) invented a new method of printing. It used metal type that could be moved and re-used over and over again in a printing press. This new method meant that lots of copies of books could be printed in a fraction of the time compared with hand-written books.

If you ever write anything down then you've probably got me, László Bíró, to thank. In the 1930s, I invented a new type of pen that used a small rolling ball to spread ink in a thin line onto the page – the ballpoint pen was born.

LÁSZLÓ BÍRÓ

Electronic communication

'Mr Watson – come here – I want to see you' were the first words spoken by Alexander Graham Bell using a telephone.

1830s – the electric telegraph is invented, carrying signals across continents and whole oceans using wires.

1876 – Scottish engineer Alexander Graham Bell (1847–1922) patents the first telephone.

S

1973 – The Motorola Company makes the first mobile phone. The first mobile phone was 25 cm long and weighed 1.1 kg.

1895 – Italian inventor Guglielmo Marconi (1874–1937) sends a radio signal over a kilometre. Six years later he sends a radio signal, the letter 'S', right across the Atlantic Ocean.

COMPUTERS AND THE INTERNET

The small smartphone you hold in your hand contains an amazing amount of computing power and can cope with millions of calculations every second. It can tell you what the time is, what weather is heading your way and, of course, it lets you make and receive phone calls. But computers weren't always this powerful or this small.

Clockwork computer
In 1837, English mathematician Charles Babbage (1791–1871) started to design an early type of computer called an Analytical Engine. Although it was never built, it was designed to solve complicated mathematical equations.

Computer coders
My name is, Ada Lovelace (1815–1852) and I saw that Babbage's Analytical Engine could be told to do different things, apart from pure calculation. I proposed a set of instructions, called an algorithm, and I am considered the world's first computer programmer.

ADA LOVELACE

During the Second World War (1939–1945), computers were used to set and crack top-secret codes. These machines, such as Colossus in the UK, were huge and filled entire rooms.

My name is Grace Hopper and in 1952, I built a device called a compiler. This was programmed with a range of commands, which it then translated into a code that a computer could understand, making programming faster and easier.

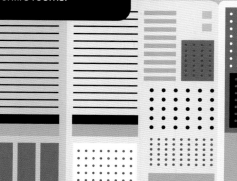

GRACE HOPPER

The microprocessor was invented in 1971. It helped to shrink computers, leading to the creation of desktop and laptop computers as well as smartphones and gaming consoles.

The Sunway TaihuLight is a modern supercomputer and one of the fastest in the world. It can handle about 93,000 trillion calculations every single second – better get your calculator ready!

Q: Who invented the internet?

A: It was developed by various American scientists and engineers to link military and scientific computers and share information. This first network, created in 1969, was called ARPANET and only four computers were linked using it.

In 1985, there were fewer than 5,000 devices linked to the internet. By 2020, it is predicted that this number will have risen to 20.4 billion devices.

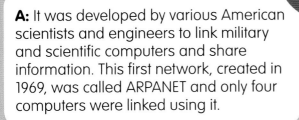

The World Wide Web is a huge collection of websites containing everything from financial information to pictures of cute cats. It was developed in the 1980s by British programmer Tim Berners-Lee as a way of sharing information inside the CERN research institute.

SOUND AND PICTURES

Whether you're on the edge of your seat in the cinema, listening to your favourite tracks as you walk along, or just chilling out in front of the TV, these are the inventions that make your downtime nice and relaxing.

Early moving pictures
In 1824, John Ayrton Paris invented the thaumatrope – a card with pictures on both sides that was spun to create the impression of a moving image.

The kinetoscope was invented by William Dickson between 1888 and 1892. It allowed one person to watch a spool of film through a small peephole.

In the 1890s, two French inventors, Auguste Lumière (1862–1954) and Louis Lumière (1864–1948), developed the cinematograph, which allowed a crowd of people to view moving pictures. They shot their first moving pictures with it in 1895, but they didn't think the technology had a future, and abandoned the film business in 1905.
How wrong they were …

Key film developments

1902 – English photographer Edward Raymond Turner records the first colour moving pictures using red, blue and green filters.

1927 – *The Jazz Singer* is the first talking film. Before then, all films were silent.

1937 – *Snow White and the Seven Dwarfs* is the first full-length animated film.

1975 – Garrett Brown invents the Steadicam, which allows film makers to record shake-free pictures.

1986 – the first IMAX theatre is built in Vancouver, Canada, to show widescreen and 3D films.

1995 – *Toy Story* is the first full-length feature film that's completely animated by computer.

THOMAS EDISON

Recording sounds

It's me again! In 1877, I invented the phonograph, a device that recorded sounds as grooves on a cylinder of tinfoil. The first words I recorded were 'Mary had a little lamb'.

Tinfoil cylinders wore out quickly, so these were replaced by wax cylinders. Then, in 1887, German-American inventor Emile Berliner developed a method of recording sounds onto flat vinyl discs, known as records. They were played using a device called a gramophone.

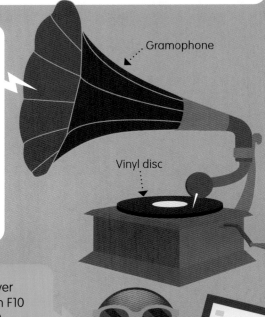

...... Gramophone

Vinyl disc ......

In 1982, technology companies Sony and Philips released a whole new way of playing sounds. Instead of using grooves, sounds were recorded digitally and stored on shiny compact discs, or CDs, that were read using lasers.

In 1998, the first MP3 player was created. The MPMan F10 could hold about 10 to 20 songs. Today's digital music players can hold thousands of songs, while some don't hold any songs at all and simply stream music over the internet.

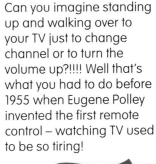

Q: Who invented television?

A: In 1924, Scottish inventor John Logie Baird (1888–1946) built the first television system, which used a spinning disc with small holes to scan an image and convert it into electric signals.

Can you imagine standing up and walking over to your TV just to change channel or to turn the volume up?!!!! Well that's what you had to do before 1955 when Eugene Polley invented the first remote control – watching TV used to be so tiring!

25

POWERING THE WORLD

Flick a switch and a light comes on. Push a button and your laptop starts up in the blink of an eye. Without thinking, you use dozens of electrical devices every day. But just how do these gadgets and gizmos get the power to work?

In 1780, Italian scientist Luigi Galvani was dissecting a frog that was held in place by a brass hook. When Galvani touched the dead frog with his iron scalpel its leg started to twitch! What was happening?!

Galvani's friend, Alessandro Volta, thought that the twitching was being caused by the two different metals being joined by a damp material and he put these ideas to good use ...

Q: Who invented the battery?

A: I am Italian inventor Alessandro Volta (1745–1827) and in 1799 I invented the battery. I built a stack of zinc and copper discs and cardboard that had been soaked in salty water – the first battery!

ALESSANDRO VOLTA

In 1859, Gaston Planté invented the rechargeable battery, using sheets of lead that were placed in sulphuric acid. **DO NOT TOUCH!**

The next challenge was to get this incredible power source into people's homes. By the second half of the 19th century, there were two camps competing to supply electricity into our living space. The competition became known as the War of the Currents, and things got pretty ugly.

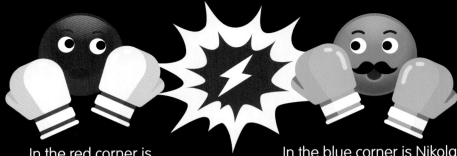

In the red corner is Thomas Edison and the Direct Current (DC) team.

In the blue corner is Nikola Tesla and the Alternating Current (AC) team.

Edison tried to discredit Tesla's alternating current as dangerous, and even electrocuted stray animals using AC to prove his point. NOT NICE!

However, several key bids were won by the AC team, including lighting up the whole city of Buffalo, USA, in 1896, and AC won the war, so our homes are powered by alternating current today.

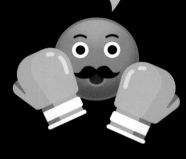

Huge demands for electricity today could lead to power shortages as suppliers struggle to keep up. One solution could be to build enormous batteries to store electricity generated by renewable power sources, such as solar, wind, and even wave power.

This is not as crazy as it sounds. In November 2017, tech billionaire Elon Musk built a huge battery complex in South Australia that's charged up by a nearby wind farm. It can provide enough energy to power 30,000 homes for a little over an hour.

A MATERIAL WORLD

The clothes on your back have come a long way from the simple furs worn by our prehistoric ancestors. Today's garments use modern artificial fibres and space-age fasteners to keep us warm and fashionable in all conditions.

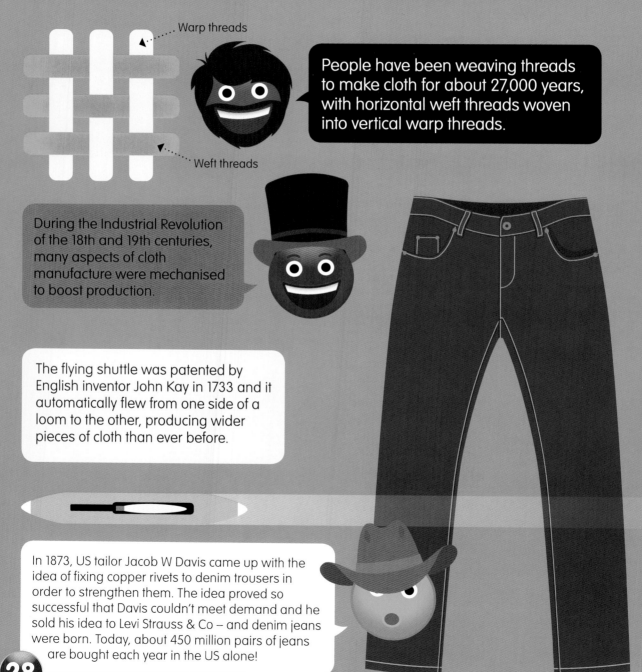

Warp threads

People have been weaving threads to make cloth for about 27,000 years, with horizontal weft threads woven into vertical warp threads.

Weft threads

During the Industrial Revolution of the 18th and 19th centuries, many aspects of cloth manufacture were mechanised to boost production.

The flying shuttle was patented by English inventor John Kay in 1733 and it automatically flew from one side of a loom to the other, producing wider pieces of cloth than ever before.

In 1873, US tailor Jacob W Davis came up with the idea of fixing copper rivets to denim trousers in order to strengthen them. The idea proved so successful that Davis couldn't meet demand and he sold his idea to Levi Strauss & Co – and denim jeans were born. Today, about 450 million pairs of jeans are bought each year in the US alone!

Plastic materials

During the 1930s, American chemist Wallace H Carothers, working with the DuPont company, developed a thin plastic fibre called nylon. This could be woven to make materials that were used in a wide range of clothes and objects, including parachutes, stockings and cookware.

WALLACE H CAROTHERS

Holding it together

It's all very well having a nice material, but how do you fix bits together and stop clothes falling off you? These clever inventions do just that:

1849 – US inventor Walter Hunt creates the first safety pin by bending and coiling a single piece of wire.

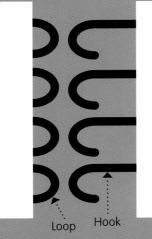

Loop Hook

1893 – US engineer Whitcomb Judson invents a device that uses a metal guide to bring together two rows of metal teeth. This first idea was then improved by Gideon Sundback in 1913 to create the zips we know and use today.

1941 – Swiss inventor Georges de Mestral has an idea for a new type of clothes fastener when he sees how the seeds of some plants stick to clothes and fur. He invents a type of fixing material with two parts – one part is covered in tiny hooks, while the other part is covered in tiny loops. The two interlock with each other when pushed together. He patented the invention in 1955 and called it 'Velcro'.

GLOSSARY

ALTERNATING CURRENT
Also known as AC, this is a type of electric current that continually changes direction as it flows.

ALTIMETER
A device fitted to an aircraft that tells the pilot how high they are flying.

ANTIBIOTICS
A type of medicine that is designed to kill bacteria and treat infections.

AQUA-LUNG
An early form of SCUBA (self-contained underwater breathing apparatus) that used a tank filled with air that was supplied to a diver through a mouthpiece regulator.

BACTERIA
Tiny living organisms, some of which can cause diseases.

BATTERY
A device that stores electrical energy in a chemical form.

COMPILER
A type of computer program that changes a language that people can understand into a code that the computer can understand.

CRASH TEST DUMMY
A human figure that is used to test how cars and other vehicles perform during a crash.

DIRECT CURRENT
Also known as DC, this is a type of electric current that always flows in the same direction.

GLIDER
A unpowered aircraft that has to be towed into the sky and can use rising air currents to lift it even higher.

HIEROGLYPHS
A system of writing that uses symbols and pictures in place of letters.

HYPOCAUST
A form of central heating developed by the ancient Romans, it used hot air that circulated under floors and between double walls.

INCANDESCENT
When a material is so hot that it glows. For example, the filament inside an incandescent light bulb.

INDUSTRIALIST
A person who is in charge of a large factory or a number of companies.

INTERNAL COMBUSTION ENGINE
A type of engine that burns fuel, such as petrol, inside itself. Most vehicles use internal combustion engines today.

JET ENGINE
A type of engine that mixes fuel and air, and sets light to this mixture to produce a blast of hot gases that shoots out of the back of the engine, pushing it forwards at the same time.

KITESURF
A small type of sailing vessel that uses a surfboard pulled along by a large kite.

KNOTS
Units used to measure the speed of planes, boats and the wind.

LED
Short for light-emitting diode, this is an energy efficient light source that produces light when electricity flows through it.

LIQUID-FUELLED ROCKET
A type of rocket that uses a mixture of liquid fuel and a liquid oxidiser to produce the blast of hot gases that push it forwards.

LOOM
A machine used to weave cloth.

MAYA
The indigenous people who have lived in Belize, Guatemala and parts of Mexico.

MICROWAVE
An invisible form of electromagnetic radiation, microwaves can be used to heat and cook food.

PENNY-FARTHING
An early form of bicycle, which featured a large front wheel and a small rear wheel.

RADAR
A system of locating the position or speed of objects, such as ships, using radio signals.

RENEWABLE POWER SOURCE
A source of energy that is naturally replaced and so, in theory, will never run out. They include solar power, wind power and hydro (water) power.

TELEGRAPH
A system of sending messages over long distances using electricity or radio signals.

VACCINATION
A type of medicine that protects a person against a disease.

VACUUM
A space that is empty of matter, even air.

VINYL
A type of hard plastic that is used to make records.

WARP THREAD
A thread that runs vertically in a piece of a woven material.

WEFT THREAD
A thread that runs horizontally in a piece of a material and is woven in and out of the warp threads.

WINDSURF
A small type of sailing vessel that uses a surfboard pulled along by a sail.

X-RAY IMAGE
A type of image that uses X-rays to form a picture of internal body parts, such as bones.

INDEX